AWARD-WINNING SPORTS BROADCASTERS

HOLLY ROWE

Tammy Gagne

Mitchell Lane
PUBLISHERS

2001 SW 31st Avenue
Hallandale, FL 33009
www.mitchelllanepub.com

Copyright © 2025 by Mitchell Lane Publishers. All rights reserved. No part of this book may be reproduced without written permission from the publisher. Printed and bound in the United States of America.

First Edition, 2025.
Author: Tammy Gagne
Designer: Ed Morgan
Editor: Morgan Brody

Series: Award-Winning Sports Broadcasters
Title: Holly Rowe

Hallandale, FL : Mitchell Lane Publishers, [2025]

Library bound ISBN: 979-8-89260-074-3
eBook ISBN: 979-8-89260-077-4

PHOTO CREDITS: cover, title page, p. 7, 11, 17, 19, 20, 23, 24, 29, 31, 35, 37, 38, 41 Alamy; p. 5, 33 freepik.com; p. 13, 27 Shutterstock; p. 14 wikimedia

CONTENTS

1	**Preparing** for the **Future**	4
2	A **Clear Vision**	10
3	A **Go-Getter** from the **Beginning**	18
4	**Beating** the **Odds**	26
5	**Working Through** It	34
	Timeline	42
	Find Out More	43
	Glossary	44
	Works Consulted	46
	Index	48
	About the Author	48

CHAPTER ONE

PREPARING FOR THE FUTURE

"Thanks for making time to speak with me, Mr. Friedman," Ava said as she opened the folder in her lap. She had prepared for this meeting. She wanted it to go well.

"You're welcome," her guidance counselor replied. "I hear that you want to take some classes above your grade level."

"Yes, sir," Ava answered. "I think that taking these classes next year will help me get into a good college." She handed Mr. Friedman a list of the courses she hoped to add to her schedule.

CHAPTER ONE

"You want to take debate, **psychology**, *and* **ethics**?" he asked.

"That's correct," she said. "I would also like to take part in the school's morning announcements if I may, reporting the outcomes and scores for all our sports teams. I'd be happy to make the arrangement dependent on getting an A or B in each of my classes."

"And what is it you want to study in college?" Mr. Friedman asked. Her requests seemed both ambitious and rather random."

"I want a degree in sports journalism," she stated matter-of-factly. "Holly Rowe—she's my idol," Ava added, "took some of these same classes as a student. She thinks that preparation is key to succeeding in this business."

She then handed her guidance counselor her most recent report card. She thought it would show him that she could handle the courses. "I've also spent the last semester working on the school newspaper," she added, handing him the newest issue.

PREPARING for the FUTURE

Holly Rowe prepared to become a sports journalist by learning everything she could about sports and reporting on them.

CHAPTER ONE

"Tell me more about Holly Rowe," Mr. Friedman then asked. "She has clearly made an impression on you.

"Oh yes, she has," Ava answered. "Like her, my favorite sport is college football. But I want to learn about all sports. Holly once covered three different sports in three different cities in twenty-four hours. And she knows her stuff. She jokes that she has a database about professional players inside her head. I'm good at remembering sports facts, too. I want to inspire other girls to go into sports journalism. More women are choosing this career. But the next generation will need their own Holly Rowes." Ava finally took a breath.

"I can see this is something you feel very passionate about," Mr. Friedman noted. "But I don't want you to overload yourself. How do your parents feel about this kind of workload?"

PREPARING for the FUTURE

"They tell me that it is important to go after the things I want in life. They also say that I must prepare and work hard for these things."

"I tell you what," Mr. Friedman offered. "I will sign off on the classes and put in a good word with the principal about the announcements. But you must add a fun elective to your schedule for at least one quarter. Maybe art or music?"

"I actually think debate class sounds like fun," Ava insisted. "But Holly Rowe plays the piano. I'll take your deal. And thank you for your help."

"That's what I'm here for," Mr. Friedman said. He then added, "I think I need to learn more about Holly Rowe. She sounds like a great role model for young people."

CHAPTER TWO

A CLEAR VISION

Holly Rowe was born in Utah on June 16, 1966. Her love of sports developed when she was a preschooler. Holly's father, Del, started taking Holly to sporting events when she was just three or four years old. She especially loved going to football games as a young girl. She has fond memories of attending college games at Brigham Young University with her father and sisters when she was just five or six.

CHAPTER **TWO**

She and her sisters didn't just watch sports. They also played sports themselves while growing up in the city of Bountiful. Holly said that sports were a huge part of the fabric of her early family life.

In the 1970s, most professional sports were played by men. And most of the fans were also male. But the Rowe household didn't worry about what other people thought. They just worried about who won the last important game. Holly is grateful for her family culture. She told the *Oklahoman*, "I didn't grow up with a lot of, 'Oh, girls can't do that.' We just did everything. I think that's one reason I'm very successful so I thank my father for that."

When Holly was in the fifth grade, she and her classmates took a test that helped reveal what they might like to become when they grew up. Holly examined her results carefully. But none of the options she saw on the page appealed to her. She wanted to be a reporter. She watched a local journalist named Shelly Thomas on the news each night. Thomas made the job look fun to Holly. She wanted to be just like the journalist.

A CLEAR VISION

Holly knew from a young age that she wanted a career in sports broadcasting.

CHAPTER TWO

Holly had enjoyed BYU football games since she was a child. As a young adult, she decided to attend the school.

A CLEAR VISION

"She was warm and friendly and classy and good at her job," Holly told the *Daily Universe*. "So I had a clear vision as a young person of what I wanted to do." It makes sense that she ended up combining her love of sports with her dream of becoming a journalist. As a teen, Holly saved newspaper clippings about BYU's victories.

Holly graduated from Woods Cross High School in 1984 before heading to BYU. A year and a half later, she transferred to the University of Utah with a **major** in broadcast journalism. She has joked that she created her own **minor** by taking classes about coaching basketball and football, sports ethics and psychology, and even sports law. She was hungry to learn everything she could about sports. Before graduating in 1991, she wrote articles for the *Daily Utah Chronicle* and the *Davis Clipper* newspapers. She even worked as an anchor for the University of Utah's TV news station.

CHAPTER **TWO**

Although few women worked in sports broadcasting at this time, Holly didn't hesitate to go after the career that she wanted. She refused to see herself differently than any other person pursuing a job in sports journalism. She told the *Oklahoman*, "I do my homework. I study hard. I try to be good and I feel like you earn respect—male or female. You're only as good as your last report, so I just try to work hard and represent myself well."

A **CLEAR VISION**

Holly didn't worry about how many women worked in sports broadcasting. Instead, she put all her effort into becoming the best sports journalist she could.

CHAPTER THREE

A GO-GETTER FROM THE BEGINNING

Holly with WNBA player Maya Moore

After graduation, Holly spent the next year as an **intern**. Basketball coach Rick Majerus had been one of Holly's instructors at the University of Utah. He wrote her a letter of recommendation when she applied for her internship at *CBS Sports*. She says that letter helped her get the spot.

CHAPTER THREE

Interning under other sports journalists made Holly even more certain that she wanted to become one herself.

A **GO-GETTER** from the **BEGINNING**

Holly still believes that internships are among the best ways to get one's foot in the door to journalism. But technology has come a long way from when Holly was getting her start. She thinks the tech that young people have access to now gives them even more opportunities to set themselves apart. Holly encourages kids to use blogs, including video blogs, to do their own stories if they are interested in reporting.

Interning wasn't glamorous work. Holly spent much of her time performing low-level tasks for journalists and other *CBS Sports* employees. But the opportunity allowed her to see what sports journalism was like up close. This made her even more certain it was the career she wanted. Her time as an intern also introduced her to many people who were willing to share their knowledge of the business with her.

CHAPTER **THREE**

Holly remembers sportscaster Lesley Visser being especially friendly and helpful during this time. Visser asked Holly if she had ever considered becoming a sideline reporter. This was how Holly learned what people who interviewed players and coaches during games were called.

In 1992, the Blue and White Sports Network hired Holly for her first full-time position in sports journalism. She worked as a sideline reporter for the network which covered BYU and U.S. Air Force basketball and football games. Whatever reporting task she was asked to do, Holly eagerly accepted.

She also saw opportunities that others overlooked. When Holly learned that ABC was planning to broadcast a BYU football game against the University of Utah, she did some checking. The network had no sideline reporter for the event. Holly volunteered for the job. Pleased with her work, ABC hired her to cover other college games in 1995 and 1996.

A GO-GETTER from the BEGINNING

Lesley Visser was one of the first female sports broadcasters. She has worked in the business for nearly five decades.

CHAPTER THREE

Holly enjoys her career so much that it often doesn't feel like work to her.

A GO-GETTER from the BEGINNING

Holly also saw an opportunity that others had missed completely. Local radio stations were carrying the men's basketball games at BYU. But no one was broadcasting the women's games. Holly used her own money to purchase air time on KALL radio so she could cover the games herself. During each game, Holly provided play-by-play coverage of the action for listeners.

Soon, Holly received an offer to start covering games for ESPN. At first, she only appeared in select broadcasts. But by 1998, she was working for the all-sports network full time.

While others saw Holly's obvious drive, she joked that she had yet to work a day in her life. She deeply enjoyed sports broadcasting, so it never felt like work to her. As she told KJZZ, "I go to work and I'm in the zone because I love what I'm doing."

CHAPTER FOUR

BEATING THE ODDS

The Running of the Bulls in Pamplona, Italy

Holly had already covered a wide range of sports when she came to ESPN. She had reported on football, softball, and volleyball games at the college level. Now her **résumé** was expanding even more.

At ESPN, she performed play-by-play announcing for the 1998 Women's World Cup soccer event. She even hosted ESPN's coverage of the Running of the Bulls in Pamplona, Italy. Far from a typical sport, this dangerous event attracts much attention each year. As part of the San Fermin festival, men and boys run ahead of a group of bulls while the fierce animals charge through the city's narrow streets.

CHAPTER **FOUR**

There didn't seem to be a sports story that Holly couldn't report. But she quickly became best known for covering women's basketball for ESPN. In addition to college games, Holly also reported on games for the WNBA, which was founded shortly before she started working at ESPN.

Viewers could feel the energy and enthusiasm that Holly brought to the games she covered. It was obvious she truly loved basketball. Holly credits a specific player with drawing her to the sport. Now a coach for the South Carolia Gamecocks, Dawn Staley played in the WNBA from 1999 to 2006. But Holly remembers watching Staley play for the University of Virginia. "I just got obsessed with the game because of Dawn Staley, and I frequently told her I wouldn't be here if it wasn't for [her]," Holly said in an interview with *Fox Carolina*.

BEATING the ODDS

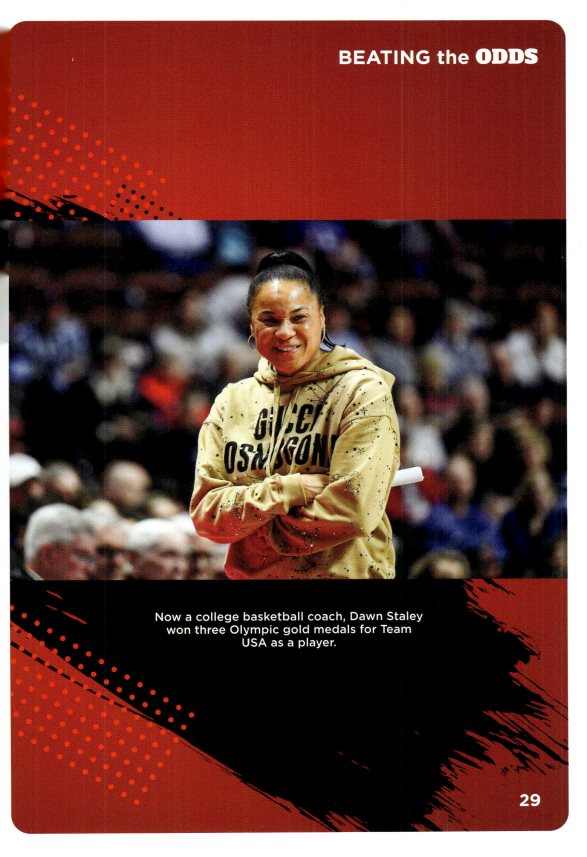

Now a college basketball coach, Dawn Staley won three Olympic gold medals for Team USA as a player.

CHAPTER **FOUR**

Holly's career at ESPN thrived as she continued to cover women's basketball for the network for more than a decade. But in 2015, a new challenge confronted her. This time, it wasn't one she had ever hoped to face. Holly was diagnosed with an aggressive form of cancer called melanoma.

As Holly prepared to have surgery, her boss asked her if it was okay to share the news of her illness publicly. Holly told her that would be fine. She didn't think most people would even notice that she was missing from the games. But when Holly woke up following her operation, she was astonished to see that she had more than 300 text messages wishing her well. In an interview with the *Cancer Support Community*, Holly shared, "I have a ton of support from coaches and players and people that I worked with that has been amazing and has uplifted me."

BEATING the ODDS

Holly didn't realize how much she would be missed when she took time off to have surgery.

CHAPTER **FOUR**

As she had always done, Holly also looked for the opportunity in her situation. She saw her illness as giving her a **platform** to tell other people about the dangers of melanoma. More than 90 percent of melanoma cases are the result of sun exposure. Holly wanted others to know how to protect themselves from the sun. Using sunscreen, for example, can reduce the risk of developing melanoma.

She also wanted them to know how important it is to see a doctor if they discover any suspicious lumps or bumps on their skin. She told the *Cancer Support Community*, "Go get it checked because every day I think about what if I had got in sooner . . . I would not be fighting for my life right now."

BEATING the ODDS

A black ribbon represents awareness of all types of skin cancer, including melanoma.

CHAPTER FIVE

WORKING THROUGH IT

As soon as Holly was well enough to get back to work, she was covering games again. In 2017, she penned an article for ESPN's *Front Row* website. She wrote, "I am still working on getting rid of this pesky cancer. My treatments continue, but I am living a beautiful and blessed existence." She went on to explain, "When people ask me why I don't take time off, I reflect and think, 'How *could* I miss all this?'"

CHAPTER **FIVE**

Holly kept reporting even as the COVID-19 virus began spreading around the world in 2019. When the 2020 WNBA season began, nearly everything but the games themselves was different from past seasons. Instead of being cheered on by fans in the stands, the teams played in isolation to help prevent the spread of the virus. As the games aired on television, even most sports **broadcasters** were kept out of the Wubble. A combination of the words *WNBA* and *bubble*, this was what many people called the IMG Academy in Bradenton, Florida, where the games took place. Holly was the only reporter allowed to cover the games in person.

When Holly arrived at the Wubble, she had to **quarantine** for seven days before she was allowed to join the players. She has said that staying in her room for this period was surprisingly difficult. A social person, she couldn't wait to join the action and start reporting on it. At a time when the news was filled with fear and uncertainty, Holly was able to bring sports fans some much-needed fun and relaxation.

WORKING Through It

Holly interviews Oregon Ducks players Ruth Hebard (left) and Sabrina Ionescu (right) in Las Vegas, in March 2020, before all WNBA games were moved to the Wubble later that year.

CHAPTER FIVE

When the Washington Huskies won the NCAA Pac 12 football championship game, Holly was on the sidelines to interview the game's MVP, Michael Penix, Jr. (right front).

WORKING Through It

A year later, the world was moving past the **pandemic**. And Holly was moving even further forward in her sports broadcasting career. In 2021, Holly became the first female color commentator for the Utah Jazz. Color commentators discuss the details of the game between the action happening on the court.

Holly has received numerous awards during her long career in sports broadcasting. In 2016, the Phoenix Mercury named her the team's BBVA Compass Bright Futures Woman of Inspiration. Vince Kozar, the team's vice president of operations called Holly "a pioneer who has risen to the top of a historically male-dominated field."

In 2022, Holly won the Mel Greenberg National Media Award from the Women's Basketball Coaches Association. That same year, Holly added a Sports Emmy to her trophy case. She won the award for Outstanding Personality/Reporter.

CHAPTER **FIVE**

She also won the 2023 Curt Gowdy Media Award by the Naismith Memorial Basketball Hall of Fame. Dawn Staley attended the ceremony. Holly was especially touched when Staley came up to her at the event and congratulated her.

What Holly still enjoys most, though, is reporting. And she doesn't plan to stop doing it anytime soon. She renewed her contract with ESPN in 2023 to continue covering college football, college basketball, college softball, and of course WNBA basketball. Shortly after signing the deal, she told the *Athletic*, "I feel like I am living my best life and I am so grateful to ESPN for letting me keep doing this."

WORKING Through It

After reporting for ESPN for more than two decades. Holly re-signed with the sports network to continue doing what she loves most.

TIMELINE

1966   Holly Rowe is born in Utah on June 16.

1984   She graduates from Woods Cross High School.

         Holly enters Brigham Young University.

1991   Holly graduates from the University of Utah with a degree in broadcast journalism.

         She begins an internship at *CBS Sports*.

1992   Holly starts working for the Blue and White Sports Network.

1995   ABC hires Holly as a sideline reporter for college football games.

1998   Holly starts working at ESPN, a job she will continue for more than two decades.

2015   She is diagnosed with melanoma and begins treatment for the disease.

2106   The Phoenix Mercury names Holly its BBVA Compass Bright Futures Woman of Inspiration.

2020   During the COVID-19 pandemic, Holly becomes the only reporter allowed to cover WNBA games from the Wubble.

2021   Holly becomes the first female color commentator for the Utah Jazz.

2022   She receives the Mel Greenberg National Media Award.

         Holly wins her first Sports Emmy for Outstanding Personality/Reporter.

2023   She receives the Curt Gowdy Media Award.

         Holly renews her contract with ESPN.

FIND OUT MORE

PRINT

Gagne, Tammy. *Malika Andrews*. Hallandale, FL: Mitchell Lane Publishers, 2024.

Huddleston, Emma. *Legends of Women's Basketball*. Mendota Heights, MN: Press Box Books, 2021.

Shaw, Gina. *What Is the Women's World Cup?* New York: Penguin Workshop, 2023.

ON THE INTERNET

CBS Sports
www.cbssports.com

ESPN
www.espn.com

WNBA
www.wnba.com

GLOSSARY

broadcaster
A person who delivers the news on television

ethics
Principles of conduct shared by members of a society

intern
A person who shadows a job for the purpose of gaining skills and experience

major
A primary field of study

minor
A secondary field of study

pandemic
A disease outbreak occurring over a wide geographical area

platform
A means of communicating an idea with a large group of people

psychology
The study of the mind and behavior

quarantine
To isolate for the purpose of limiting the spread of illness

résumé
A list of skills and job experience given to a prospective employer

WORKS CONSULTED

"20-Year ESPN Veteran to Host Annual Fundraiser for GCSC," *Cleveland Sports Commission*, n.d. https://www.clevelandsports.org/about-us/news/2023/12/04/holly-rowe-espn-reporter-and-commentator-to-host-24th-greater-cleveland-sports-awards#:~:text=Rowe%20has%20provided%20color%20commentary,the%20Running%20of%20the%20Bulls.

Aber, Ryan. "The Collected Wisdom of Holly Rowe," *The Oklahoman*, March 13, 2016. https://www.oklahoman.com/story/sports/2016/03/13/the-collected-wisdom-of-holly-rowe/60686907007.

"Class of 2023: Holly Rowe Career Retrospective," *NBA*, August 12, 2023. https://www.nba.com/watch/video/holly-rowe-career-retrospective-class-of-2023.

Deltch, Richard. "Holly Rowe Re-Signs with ESPN on Long-Term Deal," *The Athletic*, March 29, 2023. https://theathletic.com/4362601/2023/03/29/holly-rowe-espn.

Harth, Heidi. "Behind the Lens with Jazzy Analyst Holly Rowe," KUTV, March 22, 2022. https://kutv.com/news/local/behind-the-lens-with-jazz-analyst-holly-rowe.

"History," WNBA, n.d. https://www.wnba.com/history.

"Holly Rowe," ESPN Press Room, n.d. https://espnpressroom.com/us/bios/rowe_holly/#:~:text=Covering%20a%20wide%20variety%20sports,ABC%20Sports%20in%201995%2D96.

Hoole, Beth. "ESPN Reporter Holly Rowe Credits Dawn Staley for Her Love of Women's Basketball," *Fox Carolina*, March 31, 2023. https://www.foxcarolina.com/2023/03/31/espn-reporter-holly-rowe-credits-dawn-staley-her-love-womens-basketball.

"Inside the Wubble with Holly Rowe," *Indiana Fever*, September 8, 2020. https://fever.wnba.com/news/inside-the-wubble-with-holly-rowe/

"Mercury Names Holly Rowe Woman of Inspiration," August 4, 2016. https://mercury.wnba.com/news/mercury-names-holly-rowe-woi/.

Monson, Gordon. "ESPN's Holly Rowe Comes Back to Utah—with Gratitude in Her Heart," *The Salt Lake Tribune*, October 1, 2021. https://www.sltrib.com/sports/jazz/2021/10/01/gordon-monson-espns-holly.

INDEX

ABC, 22
Blue and White Sports
   Network, 22
Brigham Young University, 11,
   15, 22, 25
COVID-19 pandemic, 36
CBS Sports, 19-21
Daily Utah Chronicle, 15
Davis Clipper, 15
ESPN, 25, 27, 28, 30, 35, 40
KALL, 25
Majerus, Rick, 19
Rowe, Del, 11, 12

Rowe, Holly
   awards, 39–40
   birth, 11
   cancer diagnosis, 30
   childhood, 11-15
   education, 6, 12, 15
   sisters, 11, 12
Staley, Dawn, 28, 40
Thomas, Shelly, 12
University of Utah, 15
Visser, Lesley, 22
WNBA, 28, 36, 40
Woods Cross High School, 15

ABOUT THE AUTHOR

Tammy Gagne is a freelance writer and editor who specializes in educational nonfiction for young people. She has written hundreds of books on a wide range of topics. Some of her favorite projects have been about journalists and athletes. Tammy's other books in the **Award-Winning Broadcasters** series include *Cris Collinsworth* and *Mike Tirico*.